Have a.

May 16, 2001

Bobbi

To:...................................................................

From:................................................................

My Beautiful Broken Shell
*Words of Hope to Refresh the Soul*
by Carol Hamblet Adams

Copyright © 1998 by Carol Hamblet Adams

Published by Garborg's, Inc.
P.O. Box 20132
Bloomington, MN 55420

Illustrated by Craig Lueck
Design by Franke Design

Printed in China

# My Beautiful Broken Shell

*Words of Hope to Refresh the Soul*

by
*Carol Hamblet Adams*

Illustrated by
*Craig Lueck*

## Acknowledgments

To Linda Blackman, my good friend and
first mentor, for believing in me...

To my colleagues in the National Speakers
Association and New England Speakers
Association, for your constant friendship,
advice, and support...

To my relatives and friends who have
stood by me over the years and given me
unfailing love and encouragement...

To the many who were strong enough to
share their brokenness with me...

To Bobbie Wilkinson, my partner and
collaborator, for your tireless efforts, for
your editorial assistance, for all the laughs,
for your generous spirit, and for sharing
my dream so completely...

To my very special family at Garborg's, for
embracing this project with such loving care
and expertise, for sharing my vision...

And to the Lord, for His inspiration
and guidance...

*Thank you all for making this
book possible.*

## Dedication

To my parents, Mae and Newt Hamblet,
for giving me life, love, and the
greatest gift, my faith.

To my husband, Steve, for sharing my life...
for your inspiration, love, and total support
of all my dreams.

To Todd, Kevin, and Kristin, my greatest
treasures, for making me the proudest
and luckiest mom in the world.

And in loving memory of Emily and Rog
Adams, two of my life's richest blessings.

*The Lord is close to the brokenhearted;*
*and those who are crushed in spirit He saves.*

*Psalm 34:18*

## Preface

This book began in 1982, shortly after my husband, Steve, was diagnosed with multiple sclerosis. I was feeling frightened... discouraged...alone.

I went to the beach one day and decided to gather a few shells for my collection. The first one I picked up was a broken scallop shell, so I threw it back. But then I picked it up again and saw myself as I was at that moment... broken, too...just like the shell. God spoke to me about my brokenness, and I put His words on paper.

Over the years, this reflection has helped me and many others get through difficult times. I have published it with the hope that it will help you or someone you love...that you may find comfort in the gentle words, in the beautiful illustrations...and that, through this book, you will find hope.

My deepest wish is that you always know how truly beautiful you are...not *despite* your brokenness...but *because* of it.

With my love and prayers,

Dawn has broken on
a beautiful day here at
the ocean. I've come to
refresh my weary spirit
and to refuel my tired soul.

*I*'m so grateful for the peace and the calm of the seashore, where time stands still and unrushed...where I can see and feel the beauty all around me.

This is my first morning at
the ocean, and as I walk
to the beach, feeling
the rich, warm sand
beneath my feet,
I decide to collect
a few shells.

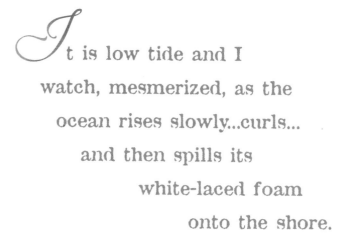

It is low tide and I
watch, mesmerized, as the
ocean rises slowly...curls...
and then spills its
white-laced foam
onto the shore.

I walk by
a broken scallop shell...
and leave it to search for
more perfect ones.

*B*ut then I stop...
go back...and pick up
the broken shell.
I realize that this
shell is me with
my broken heart.

This shell is people who
are hurting...people
who have lost loved ones...
people who are frightened
or alone...people with
unfulfilled dreams.

This shell has had
to fight so hard to keep
from being totally
crushed by the
pounding surf...just
as I have had to.

*Y*et this shell is
still out on the
beautiful sandy
shore...just as I am.

*Thank You,*
*Lord, that I haven't*
*been completely*
*crushed by the*
*heaviness*
*in my heart...*
*by the pounding*
*of the surf.*

*I*f our world
were only filled
with perfect shells, we
would miss some
of life's most
important lessons
along the way.
We would never
learn from
adversity...from
pain...from sorrow.

*Thank You, Lord,
for all that I learn
from my brokenness...
for the courage
it takes to live
with my pain...*

*and for the
strength it
takes to remain
on the shore.*

*B*roken shells teach
us not to look at
our imperfections...
but to look at the beauty...
the great beauty...
of what is still left.

If anything is still
left of me or my loved
ones, then that is
enough to grab hold of...
to keep me going...
to thank God for.

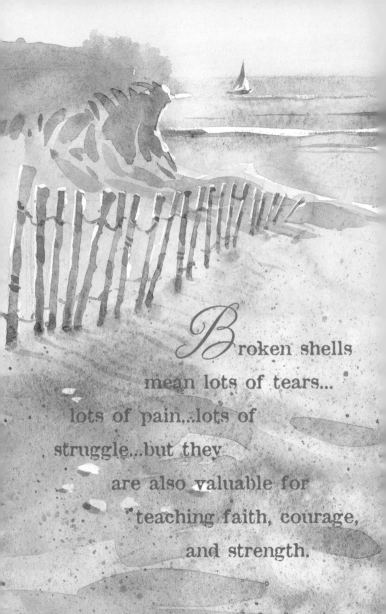

$\mathcal{B}$roken shells
mean lots of tears...
lots of pain...lots of
struggle...but they
are also valuable for
teaching faith, courage,
and strength.

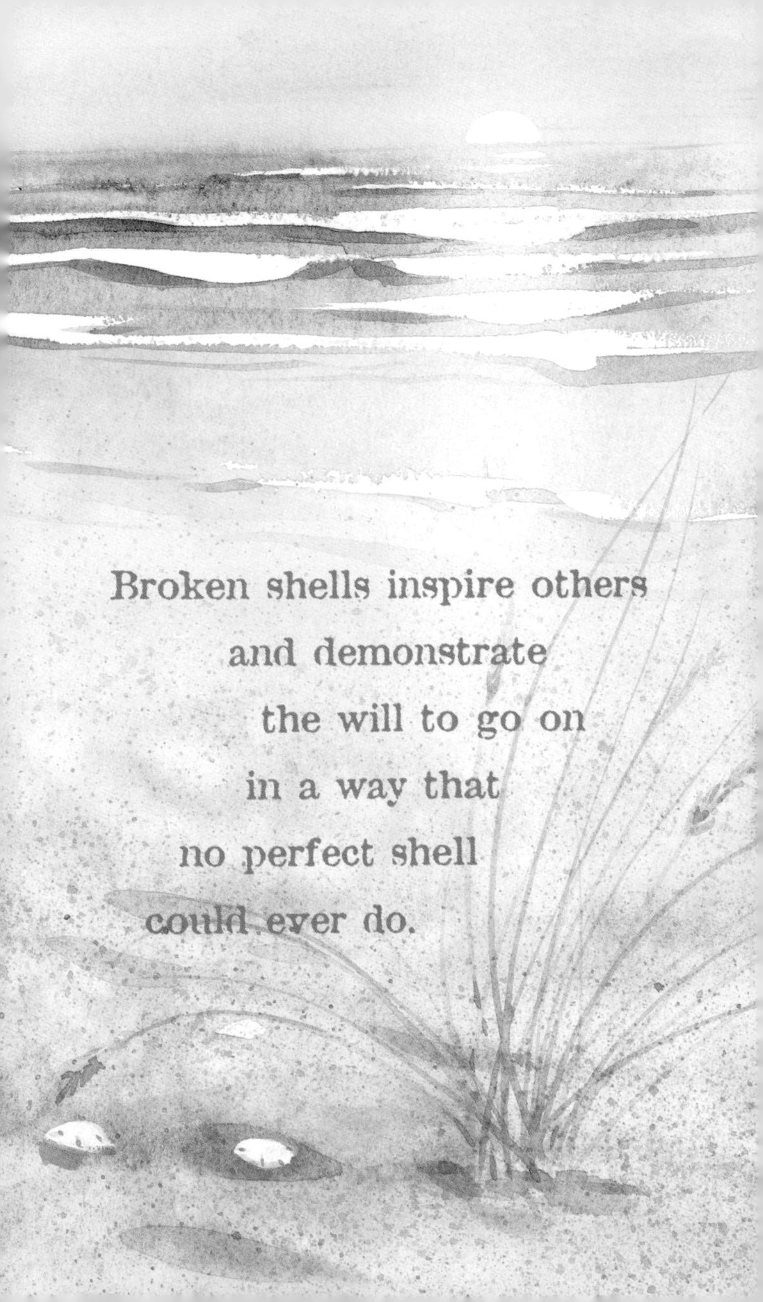

Broken shells inspire others

and demonstrate

the will to go on

in a way that

no perfect shell

could ever do.

roken shells are
shells that have
been tested...and tried...
and hurt...yet they don't quit.
They continue to be.

*Thank You, Lord,*
*for the great strength*
*it takes to simply be...*
*even when I hurt*
*so deeply that*
*there seems to be*
*nothing left of me.*

As I walk along the beach picking up shells, I see that each one has its own special beauty...its own unique pattern.

*Lord, help me to see my own beautiful pattern...and to remember that each line and each color on my shell was put there by You.*

*Help me to not compare myself to others, so that I may appreciate my own uniqueness.*

*Help me to truly accept myself just as I am, so that I may sing the song in my heart...for no one else has my song to sing... my gift to give.*

*I* watch the
rolling surf toss new shells
onto the shore, and I am
reminded of the many times
that I, too, have been tossed by
the storms of life

and worn down by the sands
of time, just like my beautiful
broken shell. But I am
reminded that broken
shells don't stand alone.

Thank You,
Lord, for being
with me to share my life...
to help me carry my burdens.

$\mathcal{T}$hank You for the
precious gift of faith that
keeps me strong when
I am weak...that keeps me
going when it would be
easier to quit.

Thank You, Lord, for
hope in times of despair...
for light in times of
darkness...for patience
in times of suffering.
For assuring me that with You
all things are possible.

wave crashes, sending
tiny sand crabs scurrying
for safety...and I am
reminded that
even the smallest creatures
depend on each other.
Especially in our brokenness,
we need the Lord...
and we need
one another.

*Thank You, Lord,*
*for filling my life with*
*people who care.*
*Thank You for my family...*
*for my friends...*
*for those who are*
*always there for me.*

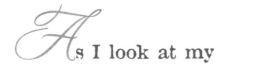s I look at my
beautiful broken shell,
I see that it has
nothing to hide.
It doesn't pretend
to be perfect or whole...
its brokenness is
clear for everyone
to see.

*Lord, may I be
strong enough to show my
pain and brokenness like
this shell. May I give
myself permission to hurt...
to cry...to be human.*

*May I have the courage
to risk sharing my
feelings with others
so that I may receive
support and encouragement
along the way.*

*Lord,* help me reach out
to others...especially to the
broken and discouraged...
not only to love them,
but to learn from
them as well.

*May I listen...*
*comfort...and give*
*unconditional love to all*
*who pass my way.*

*Lord*, help me realize
that I am not the only one
hurting...that we all have
pain in our lives. Help
me remember
that in my
brokenness
I am still
whole and
complete in Your sight.

As I walk among the many washed-up shells, I suddenly spot a broken conch shell...white and ordinary on the outside...yet brilliant coral inside.

*Lord, help
me see
inside the hearts
of the people who touch
my life...and to see
their true colors.*

*S*omehow, here at
the ocean, I receive
so many gifts.
I am grateful for
the inner peace that
fills my soul.

I take time
to notice
sandpipers playing
along the shore...
beach grasses swaying
in the salty breezes.
I delight in finding
simple treasures...a piece
of smooth green glass
polished by the waves...
a transparent white stone...
a starfish.

*Lord, help me to remain child-like in my appreciation for life. Please slow me down...that I may always see the extraordinary in the ordinary. That I may always wonder at the shell in the sand...the dawn of a new day...the beauty of a flower...the blessing of a friend... the love of a child.*

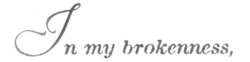

*In my brokenness,
may I never take
life so seriously that
I forget to laugh along
the way.*

*May I always take
the time to watch a kite
dance in the sky...
to sing...to pick daisies...
to love...to take
risks...to believe in
my dreams.*

As I look once more
at the broken scallop
shell in my hand,
I am reminded of all
the beautiful shells God
has placed around me.

*Lord, may I truly*
*value every moment*
*spent with my loved*
*ones while this*
*life is so briefly mine.*

*Let me not destroy
the beauty of today
by grieving over
yesterday...or worrying
about tomorrow.*

*May I cherish and
appreciate my shell
collection each and
every day...for I know
not when the tide
will come and wash my
treasures away.*

*Thank You,*
*Lord, for*
*embracing my*
*shell...whether I*
*am whole or broken.*
*Thank You for sending*
*me loved ones who care.*
*Thank You for holding*
*me in the palm of Your*
*hand...for keeping me*
*safe from the*
*pounding surf.*

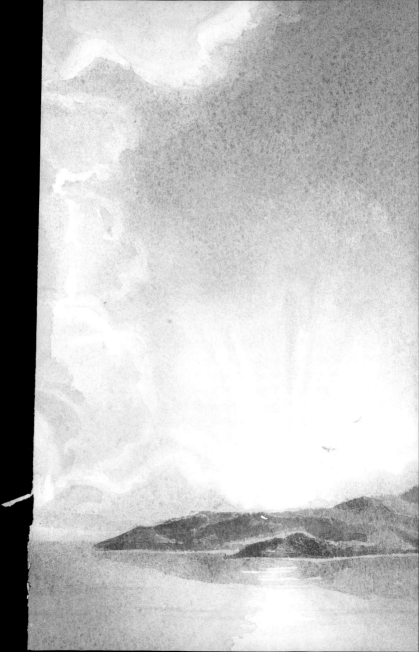

or now,
I'll just continue walking
and add to my collection
of beautiful shells.